MESSAGES FROM THE HEART AND SOUL

A Journey Through Life's Deepest Reflections

Elijah M. James, Ph. D.

Copyright © 2024
All rights reserved

No part of this book may be reproduced in any form or by any electronic or mechanical means without permission in writing from the publisher.

Canadian Cataloguing in Publication Data
James, Elijah M.
Messages from the Heart and Soul: A Journey Through Life's Deepest Reflections

ISBN 978-1-0689032-9-8

EJ Publishing
663 White Hills Run
Hammonds Plains
Nova Scotia, Canada. B4B 1W7

This book is lovingly dedicated to my sister, Vera (Star-V) who taught me to listen to the messages from the heart and soul. The profound moments that we share have touched the very core of my being and have left me forever changed.

Table of Contents

Preface 1
Acknowledgments 5

Introduction: The Quiet Echoes of Life 9
Understanding the Power of Reflection 9
The Role of Reflection in Personal Growth 10
Embracing Vulnerability and Openness 11

Chapter 1: The Innocence of Beginnings 14
Introduction 14
Childhood Dreams and Lost Innocence 15
The Impact of Early Memories 16
Revisiting the Past with a Tender Heart 17
Conclusion 18

Chapter 2: The Joy and Pain of Love 20
Introduction 20
First Love: A Heart's Awakening 21
The Ache of Love Lost 23
Lessons from Heartbreak and Healing 24
Conclusion 26

Chapter 3: The Seasons of Friendship3 27
Introduction 27
Friends Who Shape Our Souls 28
The Bitter Sweetness of Goodbyes 29

Cherishing Bonds That Stand the Test of Time 30
Conclusion..31

Chapter 4: The Unseen Scars We Bear 33
Introduction..33
The Hidden Wounds of Life 34
Forgiveness: A Path to Healing 35
Finding Strength in Our Scars 37
Conclusion..38

Chapter 5: The Burden and Blessing of Responsibility 40
Introduction..40
The Weight of Expectations 41
The Joy in Selfless Giving....................................42
Balancing Duty and Desire 44
Conclusion..45

Chapter 6: The Quiet Sorrow of Regret.......47
Introduction..47
Unspoken Words and Missed Opportunities...........48
The Lessons We Learn Too Late 49
Finding Peace in Acceptance 50
Conclusion..52

Chapter 7: The Fragile Beauty of Time 53
Introduction..53
The Fleeting Nature of Moments..........................53
The Wisdom in Aging 55
Embracing the Present with Gratitude 56

Conclusion 57

Chapter 8: The Silent Battles Within 58
Introduction 58
The Struggles We Hide from the World 58
Overcoming Inner Demons 59
The Power of Resilience and Redemption 61
Conclusion 62

Chapter 9: The Strength of Faith in Adversity . 63
Introduction: The Crucible of Adversity 63
Holding on to Hope in Dark Times 64
The Role of Faith in Overcoming Challenges 65
Finding God's Hand in Our Struggles 66
Conclusion: Faith as a Lifeline 67

Chapter 10: The Legacy We Leave Behind .. 69
Introduction: The Echoes of a Life Well Lived 69
The Imprint of Our Lives on Others 70
The Stories That Live Beyond Us 71
Building a Legacy of Love and Compassion 72
Conclusion: The Legacy of a Life Well Lived 73

Chapter 11: The Beauty of Letting Go 74
Introduction 74
The Peace in Surrendering Control 75
Embracing the Unknown with Faith 76
The Freedom in Forgiving and Moving On 77
Conclusion: The Liberation in Letting Go 78

Chapter 12: The Journey Home 79
Introduction: The Final Chapter of Life 79
Reflecting on a Life Well Lived 80
Preparing the Soul for Eternity 81
The Joyful Reunion with Our Creator 82
Conclusion: The Final Homecoming 83

Conclusion: Tears of Healing and Hope 84
The Transformative Power of Reflection 84
Embracing Life's Lessons with an Open Heart 85
Moving Forward with Renewed Purpose 86
Conclusion: A Journey of Healing and Hope 87

Epilogue: A Letter to My Younger Self 89
Words of Wisdom from the Journey 89
Encouragement for the Path Ahead 90
A Blessing for the Future 91

Preface

Life is a journey marked by countless experiences, each leaving an indelible imprint on our souls. From the innocent days of childhood to the wisdom of old age, every step we take echoes through the corridors of our hearts, shaping who we are and how we see the world. These echoes—the whispers of past joys, sorrows, triumphs, and regrets—resonate deeply within us, often in ways we may not fully comprehend until we take the time to pause and reflect.

This book, **Messages from the Heart and Soul**, was born out of a desire to explore these profound moments, the ones that touch the very core of our being and leave us forever changed. It is an invitation to journey inward, to revisit the memories that have shaped you, and to uncover the hidden truths that lie within them. It is a call to embrace the full spectrum of human emotion, to sit with both the beauty and the pain, and to allow yourself to be transformed by the lessons life has to offer.

As I embarked on writing this book, I found myself reflecting on my own life—on the dreams of my youth, the love that has both lifted me and broken me, the friendships that have sustained me, and the trials that have tested my faith. I realized that it is in these very reflections that the deepest meaning of our existence is found. It is in the quiet moments of introspection that we come to understand who we truly are, and how we have been shaped by the forces of love, loss, joy, and suffering.

This book is not merely a collection of stories or reflections; it is a mirror in which you may see your own life reflected. Each chapter is designed to resonate with the echoes of your own soul, to stir memories long forgotten, and to bring to the surface emotions that may have been buried deep within. It is my hope that as you read, you will find yourself moved to tears, not only by the beauty of the words, but by the memories and feelings they evoke within you.

Messages from the Heart and Soul is also a tribute to the resilience of the human spirit. It is a celebration of the fact that even in the face of life's greatest challenges, we have the capacity to grow, to heal, and to find meaning. The stories and reflections within these pages are meant to remind you that you are not alone in your struggles and that even the darkest moments of your life hold the potential for profound growth and transformation.

In writing this book, I have drawn inspiration from the many people I have encountered along my own journey—those who have shared their stories with me, who have opened their hearts and allowed me to witness their most vulnerable moments. Their courage and authenticity have been a constant reminder that there is great power in sharing our stories, in being honest about our fears and our failures, and in finding strength in our shared humanity.

As you turn these pages, I encourage you to read with an open heart. Allow yourself to be vulnerable, to feel the full range of emotions that this book may bring forth. Let the messages from your own heart and soul guide you as you reflect on your life, your choices, and the paths you have taken. And most importantly, allow yourself to be moved—to laughter, to tears, to moments of deep introspection.

This book is not only for those who are seeking to understand their past; it is for anyone who longs to live a more meaningful and intentional life. It is for those who wish to deepen their connection with themselves, with others, and with the world around them. It is for anyone who believes that life is more than just a series of events, but a journey of the soul—a journey that is rich with meaning, purpose, and the potential for growth.

In the end, **Messages from the Heart and Soul** is a reminder that every life is a story worth telling, and that every soul carries within it a symphony of messages that deserve to be heard. As you embark on this journey, may you find the courage to listen to the messages from your own heart and soul, and may they lead you to a place of greater understanding, compassion, and love.

Thank you for allowing me to share this journey with you. I hope that the reflections within these pages will touch your heart, as they have touched mine, and that they will inspire you to live your life with greater awareness, gratitude, and purpose.

With heartfelt sincerity,

Elijah M. James

Acknowledgments

Writing **Messages from the Heart and Soul** has been a deeply personal and transformative journey, one that I could not have undertaken alone. There are many people to whom I owe a profound debt of gratitude for their support, encouragement, and inspiration along the way.

First and foremost, I thank God for guiding me through this process, for giving me the strength to explore the depths of my soul, and for placing the right people in my life at the right moments. Your presence has been my constant source of inspiration, and I am forever grateful.

To my family, who have always believed in me and supported me unconditionally—thank you for your love, patience, and understanding. Your encouragement gave me the courage to pursue this project, and your unwavering support has been a source of strength throughout this journey. To my parents, whose wisdom and life lessons have shaped me, I owe so much of who I am. I thank them for their love and for teaching me the value of reflection and introspection.

To my friends, who have shared their stories and allowed me to share mine—your willingness to open your hearts and be vulnerable has been a true gift. Your friendship has enriched my life in countless ways, and I am grateful for the memories we have created together. You have shown me the beauty of connection, and for that, I am deeply thankful.

To the many individuals who have inspired the stories and reflections within this book—thank you for your courage and authenticity. Your lives have touched mine in ways that words cannot fully express, and I am honoured to have been able to share your experiences. Your resilience and strength are a testament to the power of the human spirit, and I hope that this book does justice to the lessons you have taught me.

A special thank you to my editor and publisher, whose guidance and insight have been invaluable. Your belief in this project from the very beginning gave me the confidence to see it through. Thank you for your dedication to bringing this book to life and for helping me shape it into something that I hope will touch the hearts of readers.

ACKNOWLEDGMENTS

Finally, to the readers of **Messages from the Heart and Soul** —thank you for taking the time to embark on this journey with me. Your willingness to explore the depths of your own soul, to reflect on your experiences, and to share in the emotions that this book evokes is what makes this work truly meaningful. I hope that these pages resonate with you and that you find comfort, inspiration, and perhaps even a sense of healing within them.

With heartfelt gratitude,

Elijah M. James

INTRODUCTION

THE QUIET ECHOES OF LIFE

Understanding the Power of Reflection

In the hustle and bustle of everyday life, it's easy to get caught up in the demands of the present moment, often overlooking the quiet whispers that linger in the background—echoes of our past experiences, thoughts, and emotions. Yet, it is these very echoes that hold the key to a deeper understanding of ourselves and the world around us. Reflection is not merely an act of looking back; it is a powerful tool for uncovering the layers of meaning within our lives, for reconnecting with the essence of who we are, and for gaining clarity on the path we are meant to walk.

The power of reflection lies in its ability to transform our experiences into wisdom. It allows us to revisit moments that have shaped us—both the joyous and the painful—and to extract the lessons they have to offer. Through reflection, we can see the patterns that have emerged in our lives, recognize the growth that has taken place, and identify the areas where healing and forgiveness are still needed. In this way, reflection becomes a bridge between our past and our future, guiding us toward a life of greater awareness and purpose.

The Role of Reflection in Personal Growth

Personal growth is often thought of as a forward-moving journey, one in which we constantly strive to improve ourselves, achieve our goals, and overcome obstacles. However, true growth requires more than just looking ahead; it demands that we also take the time to look within. Reflection is the process through which we engage in this inner journey, allowing us to connect with our deeper selves and to cultivate the self-awareness necessary for meaningful change.

When we reflect on our experiences, we gain insight into the beliefs, values, and emotions that drive our actions. We come to understand the motivations behind our choices, the reasons for our successes, and the root causes of our challenges. This understanding empowers us to make conscious decisions about how we want to live our lives moving forward. It helps us to break free from patterns that no longer serve us, embrace new perspectives, and align our actions with our true desires.

Reflection also plays a crucial role in emotional healing. By revisiting past wounds and acknowledging the pain we have experienced, we can begin the process of letting go and moving on. It is through this reflective practice that we find the strength to forgive—both ourselves and others—and to release the burdens that weigh us down. In doing so, we create space for new growth, new opportunities, and new joys to enter our lives.

Embracing Vulnerability and Openness

To truly benefit from the power of reflection, we must be willing to embrace vulnerability and openness. This means allowing ourselves to be honest about our feelings, confront the parts of our past that we may have avoided, and acknowledge the full spectrum of our emotions. Vulnerability is often seen as a weakness, but in reality, it is one of the greatest strengths we can cultivate. It is through vulnerability that we connect with our authentic selves and with others on a deeper level.

Embracing vulnerability requires courage—the courage to face our fears, to admit our mistakes, and to accept ourselves as we are, imperfections and all. It is this courage that allows us to be open to new possibilities, to take risks, and to grow beyond the limitations we have placed on ourselves. When we approach life with an open heart and mind, we become more receptive to the lessons that reflection has to offer. We become more compassionate, more understanding, and more capable of navigating the complexities of life with grace and resilience.

Openness also involves a willingness to share our experiences with others. By being vulnerable and open in our relationships, we invite others to do the same, creating a space for mutual growth and healing. Sharing our reflections, our insights, and our stories can inspire those around us and build connections that are rooted in authenticity and trust. In this way, the echoes of our own reflections can extend beyond ourselves, touching the lives of others and contributing to a collective journey of growth and understanding.

As we embark on the journey of embracing **Messages from the Heart and Soul**, I invite you to embrace the power of reflection, to be open to the lessons it has to offer, and to approach this process with vulnerability and courage. The quiet echoes of life have much to teach us if only we take the time to listen. Let this book be a guide as you explore the depths of your own soul, and may the reflections you encounter along the way lead you to a place of greater wisdom, peace, and fulfillment.

CHAPTER 1

THE INNOCENCE OF BEGINNINGS

Introduction

Every life begins with a story—a story filled with the purest of dreams, untainted by the realities of the world. The early years of our lives, often referred to as the age of innocence, are marked by an unfiltered view of life, where everything seems possible, and the world is a playground of endless wonder. It is during this time that our hearts are most open, our imaginations most vivid, and our spirits most free. But as we grow older, the innocence of these beginnings is often overshadowed by the complexities and challenges of life. Yet, it is in these very beginnings that the foundation of who we are is laid, and the echoes of these early experiences continue to shape us in profound ways.

In this chapter, we will explore the significance of childhood, the dreams that once filled our hearts, and the inevitable loss of innocence that comes with growing up. We will reflect on the impact of early memories and the importance of revisiting the past with a tender heart. Through this exploration, we hope to reconnect with the child within, to honour the dreams that once guided us, and to find healing in the acceptance of all that has been.

Childhood Dreams and Lost Innocence

Childhood is often seen as a time of boundless possibility, where the world is full of magic and every day is a new adventure. It is during these early years that we first begin to dream—of who we want to be, of the places we want to go, and of the lives we hope to lead. These dreams are pure, born from a place of innocence and unbridled imagination. They are not yet clouded by the limitations of reality, nor are they burdened by the weight of expectations.

However, as we grow older, the innocence that once coloured our world begins to fade. The realities of life start to intrude, and with them comes the gradual loss of the dreams we once held dear. We are confronted with the harsh truths of the world—disappointment, failure, and the realization that not all dreams come true. The loss of innocence is a universal experience, one that marks the transition from childhood to adulthood. It is a bittersweet process, as we gain wisdom and understanding, but also lose a part of the childlike wonder that once defined us.

Yet, the dreams of our childhood do not simply disappear. They linger in the corners of our minds, resurfacing in quiet moments of reflection. These dreams, though perhaps altered by time and experience, continue to influence the choices we make and the paths we take. They are the echoes of our beginnings, reminding us of who we once were and what we once believed was possible.

The Impact of Early Memories

The memories of our childhood have a lasting impact on who we become. These early experiences shape our beliefs, our fears, and our sense of self. They are the building blocks of our identity, laying the foundation for the person we will grow into. Whether filled with joy or marked by pain, these memories leave an indelible imprint on our hearts.

For some, childhood is a time of happiness and security, filled with love, laughter, and the warmth of family. These memories provide a sense of stability and confidence, forming a strong foundation upon which to build a life. For others, childhood may be marked by hardship, loss, or trauma. These experiences can leave deep scars, influencing how we view ourselves and the world around us. The wounds of a difficult childhood can carry into adulthood, manifesting in various ways—through fear, mistrust, or a longing for something that was lost.

Regardless of the nature of our early memories, they are a crucial part of our story. They are the first echoes that resonate within us, setting the tone for the journey ahead. By acknowledging the impact of these memories, we can begin to understand the forces that have shaped us and the ways in which we continue to be influenced by our past.

Revisiting the Past with a Tender Heart

As adults, it can be tempting to look back on our childhood with a critical eye, focusing on the mistakes made, the opportunities missed, or the pain endured. However, true healing comes from revisiting the past with a tender heart, with compassion for the child we once were. This means acknowledging both the joys and the sorrows of our early years, without judgment or regret.

When we approach our past with tenderness, we allow ourselves to heal the wounds that may still linger. We can forgive ourselves for the things we did not know or understand, and we can find peace in accepting the journey that has brought us to where we are today. By embracing our childhood memories with love and understanding, we can reconnect with the innocence that once defined us and honour the dreams that still echo within us.

Revisiting the past is not about dwelling on what was lost, but about reclaiming the parts of ourselves that we may have forgotten. It is about recognizing the strength and resilience that have carried us through the years, and finding gratitude for the lessons learned along the way. In doing so, we can integrate the wisdom of our experiences into our present lives, allowing the echoes of our beginnings to guide us with renewed clarity and purpose.

Conclusion

The innocence of beginnings is a precious gift, one that continues to influence us long after childhood has passed. The dreams we held, the memories we made, and the experiences we endured all contribute to the tapestry of our lives. By reflecting on our early years with a tender heart, we can honour the child within, heal the wounds of the past, and find strength in the echoes of our beginnings.

As we continue on this journey of self-discovery, let us remember the importance of reconnecting with our roots, cherishing the dreams that once guided us, and embracing the lessons that life has taught us. In doing so, we can move forward with a deeper understanding of ourselves and a greater sense of purpose, carrying the echoes of our soul with us every step of the way.

CHAPTER 2

THE JOY AND PAIN OF LOVE

Introduction

Perhaps it is best to begin by defining that thing called love, and to my mind, the best definition of love is found in 1 Corinthians 13:4-8:

Love suffers long and is kind; love does not envy; love does not parade itself, is not puffed up; does not behave rudely, does not seek its own, is not provoked, thinks no evil; does not rejoice in iniquity, but rejoices in the truth; bears all things, believes all things, hopes all things, endures all things. Love never fails.

The epitome of love is found in John 3:16:

For God so loved the world that He gave His only begotten Son, that whoever believes in Him should not perish but have everlasting life.

Love is one of the most powerful forces in life, capable of bringing both immense joy and profound pain. It is the thread that weaves through our existence, touching every aspect of who we are and influencing the choices we make. From the tender moments of first love to the bittersweet ache of loss, love shapes us in ways that few other experiences can. It is through love that we learn to open our hearts, to embrace vulnerability, and to find meaning in our connections with others.

In this chapter, we will explore the multifaceted nature of love—the joy it brings, the pain it can cause, and the lessons it offers. We will delve into the experience of first love, the heartbreak of love lost, and the healing that comes from understanding the deeper truths of these emotions. Through this exploration, we aim to gain a greater appreciation for the role love plays in our lives and the ways in which it shapes our journey.

First Love: A Heart's Awakening

First love is often described as a heart's awakening—a time when the world seems to come alive with new colours, sounds, and emotions. It is a period of discovery, where we experience the intensity of romantic feelings for the first time. The excitement of first love is unlike anything else, filled with the thrill of possibility and the innocence of untested emotions. It is a time of exploration, where we begin to understand what it means to care deeply for another person, to desire connection, and to dream of a shared future.

The beauty of first love lies in its purity. There are no past heartbreaks to cloud our judgment, no fears of rejection or loss. It is a time when we give our hearts freely, without reservation, and with a sense of wonder at the emotions we are experiencing. The joy of first love is intoxicating, as we revel in the newfound connection and the sense of belonging that comes with it. It is a time when we begin to understand the true power of love and its ability to transform us.

However, first love also brings with it a certain naivety. In our eagerness to embrace these new feelings, we may overlook the complexities of relationships and the challenges that come with them. We may idealize our partner, seeing only the good and ignoring the flaws. Yet, it is through this experience that we begin to learn the intricacies of love—the give and take, the joys and sorrows, and the delicate balance of emotions that come with truly caring for another person.

The Ache of Love Lost

As powerful as the joy of love can be, so too can be the pain of losing it. The end of a relationship, whether it be a first love or a later connection, brings with it a profound sense of loss. The dreams we once held, the plans we made, and the deep connection we felt are suddenly gone, leaving behind a void that can be difficult to fill. The ache of love lost is a universal experience, one that touches the deepest parts of our soul and challenges us in ways we never imagined.

The pain of heartbreak can feel overwhelming as if a piece of our very being has been taken away. It is a time of deep sorrow, where the memories of happier times can become a source of anguish. We may question ourselves, wondering what went wrong, what we could have done differently, and why things had to end. The ache of love lost is not just about the absence of the other person; it is about the loss of a part of ourselves that we shared with him or her, the loss of the future we had envisioned together.

Yet, even in the midst of this pain, there is an opportunity for growth. The experience of losing love teaches us about our own resilience, about our ability to endure and to heal. It is through heartbreak that we come to understand the depth of our emotions and the strength we possess to move forward. The ache of love lost, while painful, also opens the door to new possibilities, to new experiences, and to the potential for even greater love in the future.

Lessons from Heartbreak and Healing

Heartbreak, while deeply painful, is also one of life's greatest teachers. It is through the experience of loss that we learn some of the most important lessons about ourselves and about love. Heartbreak forces us to confront our vulnerabilities, to examine our expectations, and to reflect on the true nature of our connections with others. It is a time of introspection, where we are challenged to understand not only what went wrong, but also what we truly need and desire in a relationship.

One of the most important lessons that heartbreak teaches us is the importance of self-love. In the aftermath of a broken relationship, it can be easy to fall into the trap of self-doubt and self-criticism. We may blame ourselves for the loss, believing that we were not good enough or that we somehow failed. However, it is in these moments that we must remember to treat ourselves with kindness and compassion. Heartbreak is not a reflection of our worth; rather, it is a part of the human experience that we all go through. By embracing self-love, we can begin the process of healing, of rebuilding our sense of self, and of preparing ourselves for future relationships.

Another lesson that heartbreak offers is the understanding of impermanence. Relationships, like all things in life, are not guaranteed to last forever. People change, circumstances shift, and sometimes, despite our best efforts, things fall apart. This realization can be difficult to accept, but it is also liberating. By acknowledging the impermanence of relationships, we can approach love with a greater sense of gratitude for the moments we share, rather than clinging to the illusion of forever. This understanding allows us to appreciate the present, to cherish the time we have with our loved ones, and to let go with grace when it is time to move on.

Healing from heartbreak is a gradual process, one that requires time, patience, and self-compassion. It is a journey of rediscovery, where we reconnect with ourselves and learn to find joy and fulfillment on our own. As we heal, we begin to see the wisdom in our experiences, the growth that has come from our pain, and the new opportunities that await us. Heartbreak, while painful, is not the end of the story. It is a chapter in our lives that leads to new beginnings, to new love, and to a deeper understanding of ourselves and others.

Conclusion

The joy and pain of love are two sides of the same coin, each offering its own unique lessons and experiences. Love has the power to uplift us, to bring us closer to others, and to fill our lives with meaning and purpose. At the same time, it has the ability to challenge us, to break our hearts, and to teach us about the impermanence of life.

Through the journey of love, we come to understand the complexities of human connection, the importance of vulnerability, and the strength that lies within us to endure and to heal. The echoes of love—both the joy and the pain—remain with us, shaping who we are and guiding us on our path. As we continue on this journey, let us remember to embrace love in all its forms, to cherish the moments of happiness, and to find growth and healing in the face of loss. In doing so, we open ourselves to the fullness of life, to the beauty of connection, and to the ever-present possibility of new love.

CHAPTER 3

THE SEASONS OF FRIENDSHIP

Introduction

Friendship is one of the most precious gifts we experience in life. It is through our friendships that we find companionship, support, and understanding. These bonds are woven into the fabric of our lives, influencing who we are and how we see the world. Friendships can be as varied as the seasons—some are fleeting and vibrant, while others endure the test of time, growing deeper with each passing year. Each friendship leaves a lasting impression on our souls, shaping our character and enriching our journey.

In this chapter, we will explore the different seasons of friendship. We will reflect on those friends who have touched our lives in profound ways, the bittersweet moments of saying goodbye, and the enduring connections that remain steadfast through the years. Through these reflections, we will come to appreciate the value of friendship and the impact it has on our hearts and souls.

Friends Who Shape Our Souls

Certain friends come into our lives and leave an indelible mark on our souls. These are the friends who see us for who we truly are, who walk alongside us during our most challenging moments, and who celebrate with us in our times of joy. They are the ones who understand our dreams, fears, and desires without our having to say a word. These friendships are rare and precious, often forming the core of our social lives and providing us with the emotional support we need to navigate life's ups and downs.

These soul-shaping friendships often come at pivotal moments in our lives. They may be formed during childhood, adolescence, or adulthood, but regardless of when they begin, they have a profound impact on our personal growth and development. These friends help us see ourselves more clearly, offering insights and perspectives that challenge us to grow. They encourage us to be our best selves, to pursue our passions, and to stay true to our values.

However, even the deepest of friendships may not last forever. Life has a way of taking us in different directions—whether through physical distance, changing circumstances, or personal growth. The end of a close friendship can be one of the most painful experiences we endure, as it feels like a part of our soul is being torn away. Yet, even as we say goodbye, the memories and lessons from these friendships remain with us, continuing to shape us long after the friendship has ended.

The Bitter Sweetness of Goodbyes

Goodbyes are an inevitable part of life, and they often carry a bittersweet quality. Whether it's moving to a new city, pursuing different life paths, or simply growing apart, saying goodbye to a friend can be a difficult and emotional experience. These moments are marked by a mixture of sadness and gratitude—sadness for the loss of the day-to-day connection, but gratitude for the time spent together and the memories created.

The bittersweetness of goodbyes lies in the realization that while the friendship may be ending in its current form, the impact of that relationship will continue to resonate within us. The laughter shared, the tears shed, the deep conversations, and the quiet moments of understanding all become a part of our personal history. These experiences shape our character, influence our future relationships, and contribute to our sense of self.

Goodbyes also teach us about the impermanence of life. They remind us that all relationships, no matter how strong, are subject to change. This awareness can be painful, but it also encourages us to cherish the present moment and to fully appreciate the people we have in our lives right now. By embracing the transient nature of friendships, we can approach each relationship with a sense of openness and acceptance, knowing that even if it ends, the connection was meaningful and worthwhile.

Cherishing Bonds That Stand the Test of Time

While some friendships may be fleeting, others endure the test of time, growing stronger with each passing year. These long-lasting bonds are often characterized by a deep sense of trust, mutual respect, and unconditional support. They are the friendships that weather the storms of life—the ups and downs, the changes and challenges—without losing their strength or significance.

Cherishing these enduring friendships requires effort and commitment. Life's demands can make it difficult to maintain close connections, but those who value their friendships make the time to nurture them. Regular communication, shared experiences, and a willingness to support one another through thick and thin are essential components of lasting friendships. These relationships are a source of comfort and stability, providing a safe haven where we can be ourselves without fear of judgment or rejection.

The beauty of long-term friendships lies in the shared history and deep understanding that develops over time. These friends have seen us at our best and our worst, and they accept us for who we are. They have celebrated our successes and mourned our losses, and through it all, they have remained by our side. The bond of a long-lasting friendship is a testament to the enduring power of human connection and the importance of loyalty, love, and commitment.

Conclusion

The seasons of friendship mirror the seasons of life—each one bringing its own unique beauty, challenges, and lessons. Whether a friendship lasts for a short time or a lifetime, each one has a purpose in our journey. Some friends come into our lives to teach us, others to support us, and some to simply share in the joys and sorrows of life.

As we reflect on the friendships we have experienced, we come to understand the profound impact they have had on our lives. We learn to appreciate the friends who have shaped our souls, the bittersweetness of goodbyes, and the deep gratitude we feel for the bonds that have stood the test of time.

In the end, it is the connections we make with others that give our lives meaning and richness. By embracing the seasons of friendship, we open ourselves to the full spectrum of human experience—the joy, the pain, the love, and the loss. And in doing so, we find that our lives are made more beautiful by the friendships we have cherished along the way.

CHAPTER 4

THE UNSEEN SCARS WE BEAR

Introduction

Life has a way of leaving marks on us, some visible and others hidden deep within. While physical scars may tell a story of survival, it is often the unseen scars—the emotional and psychological wounds—that leave the most profound impact. These hidden wounds shape our perceptions, influence our decisions, and colour the way we interact with the world. They can stem from a variety of experiences: loss, betrayal, trauma, or disappointment, each leaving an indelible mark on our soul.

In this chapter, we will explore the unseen scars we bear and how they affect our lives. We will delve into the hidden wounds that many carry in silence, the power of forgiveness as a pathway to healing, and the strength that can be found in embracing our scars. By acknowledging and understanding these invisible marks, we can begin the process of healing and ultimately find strength in our experiences.

The Hidden Wounds of Life

Life's journey is often fraught with challenges that leave us emotionally and mentally scarred. These hidden wounds are not always apparent to others—they may not be visible on the surface, but they run deep within our hearts and minds. The pain of these wounds can be overwhelming, manifesting as anxiety, depression, anger, or a sense of emptiness. They might arise from a single traumatic event or be the cumulative effect of many small hurts over time.

Hidden wounds can stem from various sources: the loss of a loved one, a broken relationship, betrayal by a trusted friend, or the disappointment of unfulfilled dreams. These experiences leave us questioning our worth, our purpose, and our place in the world. Unlike physical wounds, which are often treated with immediate care, emotional wounds are frequently ignored or suppressed, leading to deeper pain and unresolved issues.

One of the most challenging aspects of hidden wounds is the sense of isolation they can create. We may feel alone in our suffering, believing that no one else can understand the depth of our pain. This isolation can lead to a vicious cycle of self-doubt, shame, and further withdrawal from those around us. The stigma associated with mental and emotional health often discourages people from seeking help, leaving many to suffer in silence.

However, recognizing and acknowledging these hidden wounds is the first step toward healing. By bringing them into the light, we begin to understand their origins and how they have shaped our lives. This awareness allows us to take control of our healing journey, rather than allowing our wounds to control us.

Forgiveness: A Path to Healing

Forgiveness is a powerful tool in the process of healing our unseen scars. It is often said that forgiveness is not for the benefit of the one who wronged us but for our own peace and well-being. Holding on to anger, resentment, or bitterness only serves to deepen our wounds, preventing us from moving forward. In contrast, forgiveness offers a way to release the pain and begin the process of healing.

Forgiveness is not about condoning the actions that caused our pain or forgetting the hurt we experienced. It is about freeing ourselves from the emotional burden that weighs us down. By choosing to forgive, we take back our power and refuse to allow the past to dictate our present or future. Forgiveness is an act of courage, requiring us to confront our pain, process our emotions, and ultimately let go of the desire for retribution.

The path to forgiveness is not always straightforward or easy. It may involve a lengthy process of reflection, understanding, and empathy. We may need to forgive others, but we may also need to forgive ourselves for mistakes or choices that have contributed to our suffering. Self-forgiveness is often the hardest form of forgiveness to grant, as we tend to be our harshest critics. However, it is essential for healing, as it allows us to move forward with self-compassion and a renewed sense of self-worth.

Forgiveness also fosters reconciliation and the possibility of rebuilding relationships that have been damaged by hurt or betrayal. While reconciliation may not always be possible or even desirable, the act of forgiveness allows us to release the hold that past grievances have on our hearts. It opens the door to new beginnings and the possibility of rebuilding trust and connection with others.

Finding Strength in Our Scars

Our scars, both seen and unseen, tell the story of our journey. They are a testament to our resilience, our ability to endure, and our capacity to heal. While we may be tempted to hide our scars or feel ashamed of them, they are an integral part of who we are. By embracing our scars, we can find strength in our experiences and use them as a source of empowerment.

Finding strength in our scars involves a shift in perspective. Rather than seeing our scars as reminders of our pain or vulnerability, we can view them as symbols of our survival and growth. Each scar represents a challenge we have overcome, a lesson learned, or a truth we have come to understand about ourselves. Our scars are evidence that we have faced adversity and emerged stronger on the other side.

Sharing the stories behind our scars can also be a powerful way to connect with others. When we are open about our struggles and the scars they have left, we create a space for others to share their own experiences. This vulnerability fosters empathy, understanding, and a sense of community. It reminds us that we are not alone in our pain and that there is strength to be found in sharing our journeys with others.

Embracing our scars also allows us to move forward with a sense of purpose. Rather than being defined by our wounds, we can use our experiences to help others who may be facing similar challenges. Our scars become a source of wisdom and guidance, enabling us to offer support, encouragement, and hope to those in need.

Conclusion

The unseen scars we bear are a testament to the challenges we have faced and the strength we have gained along the way. While these hidden wounds may be painful and difficult to confront, they are an essential part of our personal growth and development. By acknowledging our scars, practicing forgiveness, and finding strength in our experiences, we can transform our pain into a source of empowerment.

In embracing our scars, we open ourselves to healing and the possibility of a more fulfilling life. We learn to let go of the past, forgive ourselves and others, and move forward with a renewed sense of purpose. Our scars become a symbol of our resilience, reminding us that we are capable of overcoming adversity and finding strength in even the most challenging circumstances.

As we continue on our journey, let us remember that our scars do not define us, but rather, they enrich our lives with the wisdom and compassion that come from lived experience. In sharing our stories and embracing our scars, we not only heal ourselves but also offer hope and strength to others who are walking a similar path.

CHAPTER 5

THE BURDEN AND BLESSING OF RESPONSIBILITY

Introduction

Responsibility is a double-edged sword, bringing with it both burdens and blessings. It is an inescapable part of life, shaping our identities, guiding our actions, and influencing our relationships. Whether in our roles as parents, friends, employees, or community members, responsibility calls us to rise to the occasion, often demanding more from us than we might think we can give. Yet, in meeting these demands, we often discover a deeper sense of purpose and fulfillment.

This chapter explores the complex nature of responsibility, examining both the weight of expectations that come with it and the joy found in selfless giving. We will also delve into the challenge of balancing duty with personal desires, and how finding this equilibrium can lead to a more harmonious and meaningful life.

The Weight of Expectations

From the moment we are born, expectations begin to shape our lives. As children, we are expected to obey our parents, excel in school, and fit into societal norms. As we grow older, these expectations evolve, becoming more complex and demanding. We are expected to build careers, form relationships, contribute to our communities, and perhaps most challenging of all, live up to the image of success that society has crafted for us.

The weight of these expectations can be overwhelming, especially when they conflict with our personal desires or when we feel ill-equipped to meet them. The pressure to fulfill our responsibilities can lead to stress, anxiety, and a sense of inadequacy. We may feel as though we are constantly striving to measure up, fearing the consequences of failure. This burden is particularly heavy when the expectations placed upon us are not our own but are imposed by others—family, society, or even ourselves.

However, the weight of responsibility is not solely a negative force. It can also be a powerful motivator, pushing us to achieve things we might never have thought possible. The expectations we face can inspire us to grow, learn, and become better versions of ourselves.

They can lead us to discover strengths and abilities we did not know we possessed, and in doing so, help us build confidence and resilience.

The challenge lies in navigating the fine line between allowing responsibility to drive us forward and letting it weigh us down. This requires self-awareness and a clear understanding of our own values and priorities. By discerning which expectations are truly meaningful to us and which are not, we can better manage the burden of responsibility and prevent it from becoming an overwhelming force in our lives.

The Joy in Selfless Giving

While responsibility often feels like a heavy burden, it also has the potential to bring immense joy, particularly when it involves giving to others. Selfless giving—whether of our time, energy, resources, or love—can be one of the most fulfilling aspects of responsibility. When we take on the responsibility of caring for others, we experience the profound satisfaction that comes from making a positive difference in someone else's life.

This joy is often seen in the roles of parents, caregivers, and volunteers. The act of nurturing a child, supporting a friend in need, or contributing to a cause greater than ourselves can fill our lives with a sense of purpose and connection. The joy of selfless giving lies in the knowledge that our actions matter, that we are contributing to the well-being of others and, by extension, to the betterment of the world.

However, selfless giving is not without its challenges. It requires sacrifice, patience, and often, a willingness to put the needs of others before our own. This can be particularly difficult in a world that frequently emphasizes individualism and personal success. Yet, the rewards of selfless giving far outweigh the sacrifices. The relationships we build, the lives we touch, and the sense of fulfillment we gain from these acts of kindness enrich our own lives in ways that material success never can.

Moreover, selfless giving has a ripple effect, inspiring others to do the same. When we take on the responsibility of caring for others with an open heart, we become a source of light and encouragement, fostering a sense of community and shared humanity. This, in turn, creates a cycle of giving and receiving that strengthens the bonds between us and contributes to the collective good.

Balancing Duty and Desire

One of the most challenging aspects of responsibility is finding a balance between our duties and our personal desires. The responsibilities we carry—whether in our professional lives, families, or communities—often require us to make sacrifices and prioritize the needs of others. However, it is equally important to honour our own desires and aspirations, as neglecting them can lead to frustration, burnout, and a loss of self-identity.

Balancing duty and desire involves a delicate dance between meeting the needs of others and nurturing our own well-being. It requires setting boundaries, making intentional choices, and sometimes, learning to say no. This can be difficult, especially when we feel a strong sense of obligation or when others depend on us. However, maintaining this balance is crucial for our overall health and happiness.

To achieve this balance, it is essential to regularly reflect on our responsibilities and assess how they align with our personal values and goals. Are we taking on too much? Are there areas where we can delegate or seek support? Are we making time for the things that truly matter to us? These are important questions to ask as we navigate the demands of life.

It is also important to recognize that our responsibilities and desires are not always in conflict. In many cases, they can complement each other. For example, pursuing a passion or interest can make us more effective in our roles as caregivers, employees, or community members. When we take care of our own needs and fulfill our desires, we are better equipped to serve others with energy, enthusiasm, and compassion.

Ultimately, balancing duty and desire requires a deep understanding of ourselves and a commitment to living a life that is both meaningful and fulfilling. By embracing responsibility with a sense of purpose and joy, while also honouring our own desires, we can create a life that is rich in both giving and receiving.

Conclusion

Responsibility is both a burden and a blessing, shaping our lives in profound ways. While the weight of expectations can feel overwhelming, it is also a powerful force that drives us to grow, achieve, and contribute to the world around us. The joy of selfless giving and the satisfaction of fulfilling our responsibilities bring a deep sense of purpose and connection to our lives.

However, the key to a fulfilling life lies in balancing our responsibilities with our personal desires. By finding this balance, we can carry our responsibilities with grace and joy, rather than feeling weighed down by them. In doing so, we not only enrich our own lives but also positively impact the lives of others.

As we navigate the complex terrain of responsibility, let us remember that it is not just a burden to bear, but also a blessing to embrace. Through responsibility, we find meaning, purpose, and the opportunity to contribute to something greater than ourselves. And in this, we discover the true essence of a life well-lived.

CHAPTER 6

THE QUIET SORROW OF REGRET

Introduction

Regret is a universal emotion, one that quietly shadows our lives, often lurking in the recesses of our hearts. It is the quiet sorrow that accompanies missed opportunities, unspoken words, and the realization that certain moments have slipped through our fingers, never to return. Regret can be a heavy burden, a reminder of the choices we wish we had made differently and the paths we wish we had taken.

Yet, while regret can be painful, it also holds the potential for growth and transformation. It is through our regrets that we learn some of life's most profound lessons—lessons about love, forgiveness, and the importance of living fully in the present. This chapter explores the nature of regret, the impact of unspoken words and missed opportunities, and the process of finding peace through acceptance.

Unspoken Words and Missed Opportunities

Regret often stems from the things left unsaid and the opportunities we did not seize. These are the moments that linger in our minds, replaying in a loop of "what ifs" and "if onlys." Perhaps we regret not expressing our love to someone when we had the chance, or not taking a leap of faith when an opportunity presented itself. These unspoken words and missed opportunities can haunt us, leaving us with a sense of incompleteness and longing for what might have been.

The pain of unspoken words is particularly acute when it involves relationships. We may regret not telling a loved one how much he or she meant to us, only to realize too late that the opportunity to do so has passed. This can be especially difficult to bear when the person is no longer with us, leaving us with a sense of unresolved loss. Similarly, missed opportunities in our personal or professional lives can leave us questioning our decisions and doubting our ability to recognize and act on the possibilities before us.

However, it is important to recognize that regret is a natural part of the human experience. No one goes through life without experiencing moments of hesitation or doubt. What matters is how we respond to these regrets—whether we allow them to paralyze us or whether we use them as a catalyst for change.

Acknowledging our regrets and understanding the reasons behind them can help us make peace with the past. By accepting that we did the best we could with the knowledge and resources we had at the time, we can begin to forgive ourselves and move forward. In doing so, we can also learn to be more mindful in the present, ensuring that we speak our truths and seize opportunities as they arise.

The Lessons We Learn Too Late

Regret often carries with it valuable lessons—lessons that, unfortunately, we sometimes learn too late. These lessons may involve the importance of living authentically, prioritizing relationships, or taking risks when the moment calls for it. In retrospect, we may realize that the things we once deemed important—such as success, material wealth, or the approval of others—were not as significant as we thought. Instead, it is the moments of connection, love, and personal fulfillment that truly matter.

One of the most poignant aspects of regret is the realization that we cannot turn back time. The opportunities we missed and the words we left unspoken are part of a past that cannot be changed. This can lead to feelings of sadness and frustration as we come to terms with the permanence of our choices. However, it is precisely this realization that makes the lessons of regret so powerful. By understanding what we wish we had done differently, we gain insight into what truly matters to us and how we want to live our lives moving forward.

The lessons we learn from regret can serve as a guide for the future, helping us make decisions that align with our values and priorities. They remind us to cherish the present, to be courageous in our choices, and to live with intention. While we cannot change the past, we can use the wisdom gained from regret to shape a more meaningful and fulfilling future.

Finding Peace in Acceptance

Finding peace with our regrets is a journey of acceptance—acceptance of ourselves, our choices, and the imperfect nature of life. This process involves acknowledging our regrets without allowing them to define us. It means embracing the fact that we are human, and that making mistakes is an inevitable part of the human experience.

Acceptance does not mean condoning or dismissing our regrets; rather, it involves recognizing them as a part of our story. By accepting our regrets, we can begin to heal from the pain they cause and move toward a place of inner peace. This process may involve forgiveness—both of ourselves and others—and letting go of the need to dwell on what cannot be changed.

One way to find peace in acceptance is by reframing our regrets in a more compassionate light. Instead of viewing them as failures, we can see them as opportunities for growth and learning. We can acknowledge that our regrets have shaped us, teaching us important lessons about life, love, and the pursuit of happiness. By embracing these lessons, we can transform our regrets from sources of sorrow into sources of strength.

Another key aspect of finding peace in acceptance is cultivating gratitude for the present moment. By focusing on the here and now, we can prevent ourselves from becoming consumed by the past. Gratitude allows us to appreciate the beauty of life as it unfolds, even with its imperfections and uncertainties. It reminds us that each day is a new opportunity to live authentically, to connect with others, and to make choices that align with our true selves.

Conclusion

Regret is a quiet sorrow that touches every life, but it also offers a powerful opportunity for growth and self-discovery. The unspoken words and missed opportunities that give rise to regret are a reminder of the importance of living fully and authentically. The lessons we learn too late teach us what truly matters in life and guide us in making better choices for the future.

Finding peace with our regrets requires acceptance—acceptance of ourselves, our past, and the inevitability of imperfection. By embracing our regrets as part of our journey, we can transform them into sources of wisdom and strength. In doing so, we can move forward with greater clarity, compassion, and a renewed commitment to living a life of purpose and meaning.

CHAPTER 7

THE FRAGILE BEAUTY OF TIME

Introduction

Time is one of life's most precious and elusive gifts, a force that shapes our existence and defines our journey. It is both a friend and a foe—providing the space for growth, love, and discovery, while also marking the inevitable passage of moments that we can never reclaim. The fragility of time is something we often fail to appreciate until it slips through our fingers, leaving us to reflect on its fleeting nature.

In this chapter, we explore the delicate beauty of time, its transient nature, and the wisdom that comes with aging. We will also delve into the importance of embracing the present moment with gratitude, recognizing that every second is a treasure, a part of our unfolding story.

The Fleeting Nature of Moments

Life is a collection of moments, each one unique and irreplaceable. These moments—whether joyful, sorrowful, or mundane—form the tapestry of our lives. Yet, despite their significance, they are fleeting, slipping away as quickly as they arrive. We often find ourselves yearning to hold onto these moments, to freeze time, but the very essence of life is change, and with it comes the passing of time.

The fleeting nature of moments teaches us the importance of presence. It reminds us that life is happening now, in this very instant, and that to truly live, we must engage with the present rather than dwell on the past or anxiously anticipate the future. The moments we cherish most—the laughter shared with loved ones, the quiet reflection at dawn, the simple joys of daily life—are the ones where we are fully present, fully alive.

This awareness of time's fleeting nature can also bring a sense of urgency, prompting us to live with intention and purpose. It encourages us to prioritize what truly matters, to spend our time on what brings us joy, meaning, and connection. When we recognize that our moments are finite, we are more likely to invest them wisely, to live in a way that reflects our deepest values and desires.

The Wisdom in Aging

As we journey through life, the passage of time brings with it the inevitable process of aging. For some, aging is met with resistance, a reluctance to accept the changes that come with it. But within the process of aging lies a profound wisdom—a wisdom that can only be gained through the accumulation of experiences, challenges, and lessons learned.

With age comes perspective. The concerns that once seemed so pressing in our youth often fade into the background as we gain a broader view of life's complexities. We begin to understand that life is not just about achieving goals or accumulating successes, but about the relationships we build, the love we give and receive, and the inner peace we cultivate.

The wisdom of aging also includes an acceptance of life's impermanence. We come to terms with the reality that time is limited and that each day is a gift. This realization can bring a deeper appreciation for life's simple pleasures—a walk in nature, a conversation with a friend, the beauty of a sunset. It can also inspire us to share our knowledge and experiences with others, to leave a legacy of wisdom and love for future generations.

Aging, then, is not something to be feared, but embraced. It is a testament to a life lived, to the countless moments that have shaped us into who we are. By honouring the wisdom that comes with age, we can approach the later stages of life with grace, dignity, and a deep sense of fulfillment.

Embracing the Present with Gratitude

Gratitude is the key to unlocking the beauty of the present moment. It is the practice of recognizing and appreciating the gifts that life offers, no matter how small or seemingly insignificant. When we cultivate gratitude, we shift our focus from what we lack to what we have, from the regrets of the past to the blessings of the present.

Embracing the present with gratitude involves slowing down, taking the time to notice the world around us, and savouring the experiences that make life rich and meaningful. It is about finding joy in the ordinary—in a warm cup of tea, the sound of birds singing, the feel of the sun on our skin. These are the moments that, when strung together, create a life of contentment and peace.

Gratitude also helps us to live more fully in the present, free from the distractions of worry and regret. When we are grateful, we are more likely to be fully engaged in our lives, to connect deeply with others, and to experience a sense of well-being and fulfillment. By focusing on the present with an attitude of gratitude, we can transform even the most challenging moments into opportunities for growth and learning.

Moreover, gratitude fosters a sense of humility and acceptance. It reminds us that life is a gift, that our time here is temporary, and that we are part of something larger than ourselves. This perspective can help us to navigate life's ups and downs with grace, knowing that each experience, whether joyful or painful, is part of our journey.

Conclusion

The fragility of time is both a challenge and a blessing. It calls us to live with awareness, to appreciate the moments that make up our lives, and to embrace the wisdom that comes with aging. By recognizing the fleeting nature of time, we are reminded to live fully, to cherish the present, and to approach life with an attitude of gratitude.

In this chapter, we have explored the beauty and complexity of time, the lessons it teaches us, and the importance of living with intention and purpose. As we continue our journey, may we carry with us the wisdom of time, the joy of the present moment, and the deep appreciation for the gift of life.

CHAPTER 8

THE SILENT BATTLES WITHIN

Introduction

Life is a journey filled with both external and internal challenges. While the external struggles are often visible to others, the battles we fight within ourselves remain hidden from the world. These silent battles—whether they involve self-doubt, fear, or pain—are no less real or significant. They shape our identity, influence our decisions, and determine our ability to overcome obstacles.

In this chapter, we delve into the nature of these silent battles, exploring the struggles we keep hidden, the inner demons we confront, and the resilience required to rise above them. Ultimately, we find that within the quiet strength of the human spirit lies the power to heal, transform, and emerge victorious.

The Struggles We Hide from the World

Each person carries within himself/herself a private world of thoughts, emotions, and experiences that are often shielded from the eyes of others. These hidden struggles can take many forms—anxiety, depression, guilt, or unfulfilled desires. They can stem from past traumas, unmet expectations, or the fear of failure. Because these battles are fought internally, they are easy to conceal, making it difficult for others to see the pain or turmoil we may be experiencing.

The decision to hide these struggles often comes from a desire to protect ourselves or others, or from the belief that vulnerability is a sign of weakness. We may fear judgment, rejection, or pity, and so we build walls around our hearts, masking our true emotions. Yet, this concealment can lead to a sense of isolation, as we carry the weight of our burdens alone.

Acknowledging these struggles is the first step towards healing. It requires honesty with oneself and the courage to confront the emotions that we have kept suppressed. By bringing these battles into the light, we can begin to understand them, address their root causes, and take steps toward recovery.

Overcoming Inner Demons

Inner demons are the fears, doubts, and negative thoughts that haunt us from within. They are the voices that tell us we are not good enough, that we will fail, or that we are unworthy of love and happiness. These demons can be powerful and persuasive, causing us to question our abilities, undermine our confidence, and sabotage our efforts to move forward.

Overcoming these inner demons requires a deep and sustained effort. It involves challenging the negative beliefs we hold about ourselves, replacing them with affirmations of our worth and potential. It requires self-compassion, the ability to forgive ourselves for past mistakes, and the willingness to embrace our imperfections.

One of the most effective ways to combat inner demons is through mindfulness and self-awareness. By observing our thoughts without judgment, we can begin to recognize the patterns of negativity that arise and learn to interrupt them. We can also develop coping strategies, such as meditation, journaling, or seeking support from trusted friends or professionals.

It is important to remember that overcoming inner demons is not a one-time event but an ongoing process. It requires patience, persistence, and the recognition that setbacks are a natural part of the journey. Each time we confront and conquer a demon, we strengthen our resilience and move closer to becoming the person we are meant to be.

The Power of Resilience and Redemption

Resilience is the capacity to recover from difficulties and emerge stronger on the other side. It is the inner strength that allows us to persevere in the face of adversity, to keep going when the road is rough, and to find hope even in the darkest of times. Resilience is not about avoiding challenges, but about embracing them as opportunities for growth.

The power of resilience lies in its ability to transform suffering into strength. When we face our silent battles with courage and determination, we develop a deeper understanding of ourselves and a greater appreciation for life's blessings. We learn to navigate challenges with grace, to adapt to change, and to find meaning in our struggles.

Redemption is the process of reclaiming our lives from the grip of our inner demons. It is the act of forgiving ourselves and others, of letting go of the past, and of choosing to live with purpose and integrity. Redemption is not about erasing our mistakes or pretending our pain never existed; it is about acknowledging our wounds and using them as a foundation for building a better future.

The journey of resilience and redemption is one of healing and transformation. It is a journey that requires faith in oneself, in others, and in a higher power. It is a journey that teaches us that no matter how deep our wounds or how fierce our battles, we have the strength to rise, to heal, and to find peace.

Conclusion

The silent battles within are some of the most difficult challenges we face in life. They test our strength, our courage, and our resolve. Yet, within these battles lies the potential for profound growth and transformation. By acknowledging our struggles, confronting our inner demons, and embracing the power of resilience and redemption, we can emerge from these battles stronger, wiser, and more compassionate.

In this chapter, we have explored the nature of our internal struggles and the path to overcoming them. May these reflections serve as a reminder that we are not alone in our battles, and that within each of us lies the strength to overcome, to heal, and to live a life of purpose and peace.

CHAPTER 9

THE STRENGTH OF FAITH IN ADVERSITY

Introduction: The Crucible of Adversity

Adversity is an inevitable part of life. It comes in many forms—illness, loss, disappointment, and unexpected challenges that test our strength and resilience. In these moments of hardship, we are often pushed to our limits, and forced to confront our deepest fears and doubts. Yet, it is also in these moments that the strength of our faith is revealed. Faith provides us with a foundation to stand upon when everything else seems to crumble. It is the light that guides us through the darkest valleys and the anchor that holds us steady in the storm.

In this chapter, we will explore the profound strength that faith offers in times of adversity. We will delve into the power of hope, the role of faith in overcoming challenges, and the ways in which we can find God's presence in our struggles. Through these reflections, we will see that faith is not just a belief, but a source of strength and comfort that sustains us through life's most difficult moments.

Holding on to Hope in Dark Times

The Elusiveness of Hope

When adversity strikes, it can feel as though the world has been turned upside down. The future, once clear and promising, becomes clouded with uncertainty and fear. In these dark times, hope can be elusive, slipping away as doubt and despair take hold. Yet, it is precisely in these moments that hope becomes most crucial.

The Choice to Hope

Hope is the belief that, despite the difficulties we face, better days lie ahead. It is the conviction that no matter how deep the darkness, the dawn will come. Holding on to hope does not mean ignoring the pain or pretending that everything is fine. Rather, it is a conscious choice to focus on the possibility of healing, restoration, and renewal. It is the decision to trust that, even when we cannot see the way forward, there is a path that leads to light.

Nurturing Hope Amidst Suffering

To nurture hope in dark times, we must turn our attention to the small signs of grace that appear even in the midst of suffering—a kind word, a helping hand, a moment of peace. These glimpses of goodness remind us that we are not alone, that there is beauty and love in the world, even when life feels overwhelming. By holding on to hope, we keep our hearts open to the possibility of joy, even in the face of adversity.

The Role of Faith in Overcoming Challenges

Faith as a Source of Strength

Faith plays a central role in our ability to overcome challenges. It gives us the courage to face our fears, the strength to endure hardship, and the wisdom to navigate uncertainty. Faith is not just a passive belief, but an active force that empowers us to take steps forward, even when the road is difficult.

Shifting Perspective Through Faith

One of the most powerful aspects of faith is its ability to shift our perspective. When we face challenges, it is easy to become consumed by the immediate difficulties and lose sight of the bigger picture. Faith helps us to see beyond the present moment, to trust that there is a greater purpose at work, even when we cannot fully understand it. This shift in perspective allows us to approach our struggles with a sense of calm and determination, knowing that we are part of something larger than ourselves.

Drawing Strength from Divine Support

Faith also connects us to a source of strength that is greater than our own. When we feel weak or overwhelmed, faith reminds us that we do not have to rely solely on our own abilities. We can draw on the strength of God, who is always with us, guiding us and supporting us through every trial. This reliance on divine strength allows us to persevere, even when our own resources are depleted.

Finding God's Hand in Our Struggles

The Hidden Presence of God

In times of adversity, it can be difficult to see God's presence. We may question why we are suffering or wonder where God is in the midst of our pain. Yet, it is often in these very struggles that God's hand is most active, working in ways that we may not immediately recognize.

Recognizing Signs of Divine Presence

Finding God's hand in our struggles requires a shift in perspective. Instead of focusing solely on the pain and difficulties, we must look for the signs of God's presence—the moments of grace, the unexpected blessings, and the strength that sustains us when we feel we cannot go on. These signs may be small or subtle, but they are there, reminding us that we are not alone.

God's Love Manifested Through Others

God's hand may also be seen in the people He places in our lives during difficult times. A friend who offers a listening ear, a stranger who provides a word of encouragement, a loved one who stands by us—these are all manifestations of God's love and care, reaching out to us through others.

Trusting God's Ways and Timing

It is important to remember that God's ways are not always our ways, and His timing is not always our timing. We may not understand why we are facing certain challenges or why our prayers seem to go unanswered. But faith calls us to trust that God is at work, even in the midst of our struggles, bringing about a greater good that we may not yet see.

Conclusion: Faith as a Lifeline

Adversity is a test of our strength, resilience, and faith. It challenges us to confront our fears, to endure pain, and to seek meaning in the midst of suffering. Yet, through faith, we find the strength to persevere, the hope to keep going, and the assurance that we are never alone.

In this chapter, we have explored the power of faith in adversity—how it sustains us, empowers us, and reveals God's presence in our lives. May these reflections serve as a reminder that, no matter how difficult our trials, faith is the foundation that carries us through, offering hope, strength, and peace in every season of life.

CHAPTER 10

THE LEGACY WE LEAVE BEHIND

Introduction: The Echoes of a Life Well Lived

Every life, no matter how ordinary it may seem, leaves a legacy. As we journey through life, the choices we make, the values we uphold, and the relationships we nurture create ripples that extend far beyond our immediate existence. These ripples form the legacy we leave behind—a legacy that continues to resonate in the hearts and minds of those we touch.

In this chapter, we will explore the concept of legacy, not as a grand monument to personal achievements, but as the enduring influence we have on others. We will examine how the imprint of our lives, the stories we share, and the love and compassion we offer can shape the world long after we are gone. This chapter invites you to reflect on the legacy you are building and to consider how you can leave a lasting, positive impact on those around you.

The Imprint of Our Lives on Others

The Power of Influence

Every interaction we have, no matter how small, leaves an imprint on the people we encounter. Whether through our words, actions, or mere presence, we influence others in ways we may never fully realize. Our kindness, generosity, and integrity can inspire and uplift, while our shortcomings and mistakes can serve as lessons and warnings. This influence forms a key part of our legacy, as it shapes the lives of those we touch.

The Subtle Imprints

Often, it is the small, seemingly insignificant moments that leave the deepest marks. A word of encouragement offered in a time of need, a smile shared with a stranger, a gesture of support during a difficult period—these are the quiet, subtle ways in which we leave our imprint on others. Though they may go unnoticed at the time, these moments accumulate to form the tapestry of our legacy.

Conscious Living, Conscious Legacy

To leave a positive imprint on others, we must live consciously. This means being aware of the impact our actions have, choosing to act with intention, and striving to embody the values we hold dear. By living in alignment with our principles, we ensure that the legacy we leave is one of goodness, integrity, and love.

The Stories That Live Beyond Us

The Power of Stories

Stories are the vessels through which legacies are passed down. The stories we share—of our struggles, triumphs, joys, and sorrows—become a part of the collective memory of those we leave behind. These stories shape how we are remembered and how our lives are interpreted by future generations.

Creating Meaning Through Storytelling

Sharing our stories is an act of legacy-building. By openly recounting our experiences, we offer others the opportunity to learn from our lives. Our stories can provide comfort, offer wisdom, and inspire those who hear them. Whether through spoken words, written accounts, or the memories we leave with others, storytelling is a powerful way to ensure that our legacy endures.

The Enduring Impact of Shared Wisdom

The wisdom we impart through our stories has the potential to outlast us. When we share lessons learned from our experiences, we contribute to the growth and understanding of others. These lessons, passed down through stories, become a part of the fabric of society, influencing future generations and shaping the world in ways we may never see.

Building a Legacy of Love and Compassion

The Foundation of Love

At the heart of any meaningful legacy is love. The love we give—whether to family, friends, or even strangers—forms the foundation of a legacy that truly matters. Love is the most enduring gift we can offer, and it is through love that our lives continue to have an impact long after we are gone.

Acts of Compassion

Compassion is love in action. When we show compassion to others, we extend our love beyond ourselves and contribute to the well-being of the world. Acts of compassion, whether grand or small, create a ripple effect that can change lives and communities. A legacy built on compassion is one that fosters kindness, understanding, and unity.

Living with Purpose

To build a legacy of love and compassion, we must live with purpose. This means prioritizing relationships, valuing kindness, and making a conscious effort to contribute positively to the world around us. By living with purpose, we create a legacy that reflects our deepest values and ensures that our lives have a lasting, meaningful impact.

Conclusion: The Legacy of a Life Well Lived

As we reach the end of our journey, the legacy we leave behind becomes our final gift to the world. It is not measured by wealth, fame, or achievements, but by the love we have shared, the lives we have touched, and the values we have upheld. A legacy of love, compassion, and integrity is one that endures, leaving an indelible mark on the hearts of those we leave behind.

In this chapter, we have reflected on the importance of building a legacy that transcends our physical existence. We have explored how the imprint of our lives, the stories we share, and the love and compassion we offer create a lasting impact on the world. May these reflections inspire you to live each day with intention, to leave a legacy that reflects the best of who you are, and to know that your life, in all its beauty and complexity, will continue to resonate long after you are gone.

CHAPTER 11

THE BEAUTY OF LETTING GO

Introduction

In life, we often find ourselves clinging tightly to things—relationships, dreams, fears, and even our own sense of control. This attachment, though understandable, can become a burden, weighing us down and preventing us from moving forward. Letting go, however, is not about giving up; it is about releasing what no longer serves us, creating space for growth, peace, and new possibilities.

In this chapter, we will explore the profound beauty that lies in the act of letting go. We will delve into the peace that comes with surrendering control, the courage required to embrace the unknown with faith, and the liberation found in forgiving and moving on. Letting go is not a sign of weakness, but a testament to our strength and resilience—a path to true freedom.

The Peace in Surrendering Control

The Illusion of Control

Many of us live under the illusion that we can control every aspect of our lives. We plan meticulously, make decisions with careful consideration, and often try to orchestrate outcomes to fit our desires. While planning and preparation have their place, the truth is that much of life is beyond our control. Holding on too tightly to the need for control can lead to stress, anxiety, and disappointment.

The Power of Surrender

Surrendering control is not about giving up; it is about recognizing the limits of our power and placing our trust in a higher force. When we release the need to control everything, we open ourselves to the flow of life, allowing it to unfold as it is meant to. This surrender brings a deep sense of peace, as we no longer feel the weight of trying to manage the uncontrollable.

Finding Peace in Acceptance

Acceptance is a key component of surrender. By accepting life as it is, rather than as we wish it to be, we free ourselves from the constant struggle against reality. This acceptance does not mean passivity; rather, it is an active choice to embrace life, with all its uncertainties and imperfections, and to find peace within that embrace.

Embracing the Unknown with Faith

The Fear of the Unknown

One of the greatest challenges in letting go is the fear of the unknown. The future is uncertain, and stepping into it without the security of control can be daunting. This fear often keeps us trapped in situations, relationships, or mindsets that no longer serve us, simply because the known feels safer than the unknown.

Faith as a Guiding Light

Faith is the antidote to the fear of the unknown. When we have faith—whether in God, the universe, or the inherent goodness of life—we are able to step into the unknown with confidence. Faith does not eliminate fear, but it gives us the strength to move forward despite it, trusting that we will be guided and supported along the way.

The Growth in Uncertainty

Embracing the unknown with faith allows for personal growth. Uncertainty can be a powerful teacher, showing us the limits of our control and the boundless possibilities that exist beyond those limits. When we let go of the need to know everything, we open ourselves to new experiences, insights, and opportunities that we might never have encountered otherwise.

The Freedom in Forgiving and Moving On

The Weight of Unforgiveness

Holding on to past hurts, grudges, and resentments can be one of the heaviest burdens we carry. Unforgiveness traps us in a cycle of pain, preventing us from healing and moving forward. It ties us to the very things we wish to be free of, making it impossible to fully embrace the present or the future.

The Healing Power of Forgiveness

Forgiveness is a powerful act of letting go. It does not mean condoning the wrongs done to us, nor does it require reconciliation with those who have hurt us. Rather, forgiveness is about freeing ourselves from the hold that past pain has on us. It is an act of self-liberation, allowing us to move forward without the burden of bitterness or anger.

Moving On with Grace

Once we have forgiven, the next step is to move on. This does not mean forgetting what has happened, but rather choosing to no longer be defined by it. Moving on with grace means carrying forward the lessons learned, while leaving behind the pain. It is an act of self-compassion, a way of honouring our own journey by not allowing the past to dictate our future.

Conclusion: The Liberation in Letting Go

Letting go is a process, one that requires courage, faith, and self-compassion. It is not always easy, but the rewards are profound. By surrendering control, embracing the unknown, and forgiving both ourselves and others, we free ourselves from the burdens that hold us back. In this liberation, we find peace, growth, and a deeper connection to the beauty of life.

As we let go of what no longer serves us, we make space for new possibilities, new joys, and new understandings. The beauty of letting go lies in the freedom it brings—the freedom to live fully, to love deeply, and to embrace the ever-changing, ever-unfolding journey of life.

CHAPTER 12

THE JOURNEY HOME

Introduction: The Final Chapter of Life

Life is a journey, a series of experiences, lessons, and moments that shape who we are and how we live. But every journey has an end, a point where we transition from this world to the next. The thought of this final chapter can evoke a mix of emotions—fear, sadness, peace, and even joy. In this chapter, we explore the journey home, the path that leads us to our eternal resting place, and the profound peace that comes with embracing this inevitable part of life.

The journey home is not just about the physical end of life; it is a spiritual voyage, a return to the Creator who gave us life. It is a time for reflection, for preparing the soul for eternity, and for finding comfort in the knowledge that death is not the end but a new beginning—a joyful reunion with our Creator.

Reflecting on a Life Well Lived

The Importance of Reflection

As we near the end of our earthly journey, reflection becomes a vital part of our experience. Looking back on the life we have lived allows us to see the impact we have made, the love we have shared, and the lessons we have learned. It is a time to acknowledge the trials and triumphs, the sorrows and joys, and to find peace in knowing that our life has been meaningful.

Gratitude for the Journey

Reflecting on a life well lived often brings a sense of gratitude. Gratitude for the people who have touched our lives, for the experiences that have shaped us, and for the opportunities we have had to grow, love, and give. This gratitude is not just for the good times, but also for the challenges, as they have helped us become who we are.

Letting Go with Peace

In reflecting on our lives, we may also recognize the need to let go of regrets, unresolved conflicts, or unfulfilled dreams. This letting go is an essential part of the journey home, allowing us to find peace in our hearts and minds as we prepare for the transition to the next phase of existence.

Preparing the Soul for Eternity

The Spiritual Preparation

As we approach the end of our earthly life, the preparation of the soul becomes paramount. This is a time to seek reconciliation, both with others and with ourselves, to ask for forgiveness where needed, and to offer forgiveness to those who have wronged us. It is a time to deepen our relationship with God, to seek His guidance, and to strengthen our faith. We ought not to wait until we think we are approaching the end of our earthly life to do these things, but this time gives us an opportunity to do them.

Embracing the Unknown

Death is the great unknown, and it is natural to feel apprehensive about what lies beyond. However, by preparing our souls for eternity, we can face the unknown with courage and faith. This preparation involves letting go of our earthly attachments and trusting that there is something greater waiting for us—a place of peace, love, and eternal joy.

The Role of Faith in Preparation

Faith is the foundation upon which our preparation for eternity is built. It is faith that reassures us that death is not the end but a transition to a new and better life. By holding on to our faith, we can face the journey home with confidence, knowing that God is with us every step of the way.

The Joyful Reunion with Our Creator

The Promise of Reunion

One of the most comforting aspects of the journey home is the promise of a joyful reunion with our Creator. After a life spent in service, love, and faith, the thought of being welcomed into God's presence brings immense peace and joy. This reunion is the culmination of our earthly journey, the moment when we finally return to the source of all life.

The Peace of Eternal Rest

In this joyful reunion, we find the peace of eternal rest. All the struggles, pain, and sorrows of earthly life will be left behind, replaced by the eternal joy of being in God's presence. This rest is not just an end, but a new beginning—a life free from suffering, filled with love, and spent in the presence of our Creator.

The Hope of Resurrection

The reunion with our Creator also brings the hope of resurrection, the promise that we will be raised to new life, just as Christ was raised from the dead. This hope gives us the strength to face the journey home without fear, knowing that death is not the end, but a passage to eternal life.

Conclusion: The Final Homecoming

The journey home is a profound and sacred part of life, a time of reflection, preparation, and joyful anticipation. As we prepare to leave this world, we do so with the knowledge that we are returning to our true home—a place of eternal peace, love, and joy in the presence of our Creator.

In this final homecoming, we find the culmination of all that we have lived, loved, and learned. It is the ultimate fulfillment of our journey, the moment when we are reunited with the One who created us and loved us through every step of our earthly life.

The journey home is not something to be feared but embraced, for it is the path that leads us to eternal life and the joy of being with God forever.

CONCLUSION

TEARS OF HEALING AND HOPE

The Transformative Power of Reflection

Life is a series of moments, each carrying its own weight of joy, sorrow, love, and loss. As we journey through these experiences, reflection becomes a powerful tool for transformation. It allows us to pause and look back on the path we've walked, to see the scars we've gained and the wisdom we've earned. In these moments of quiet reflection, we often find tears—tears that cleanse, heal, and renew.

These tears are not just expressions of sadness or regret; they are the evidence of a soul deeply touched by life's beauty and complexity. They reflect the depth of our experiences, the love we've shared, the losses we've endured, and the growth we've achieved. Reflection opens our eyes to the truths that were hidden in the busyness of daily life. It allows us to see our journey with clarity, acknowledging both our strengths and our vulnerabilities.

Through reflection, we find healing. We begin to understand that our pain, our struggles, and even our failures are not just random occurrences but integral parts of our growth. They have shaped us, refined us, and made us more compassionate, empathetic, and resilient. The tears shed during reflection are tears of healing—releasing the old wounds, forgiving the past, and making space for new beginnings.

Embracing Life's Lessons with an Open Heart

Life teaches us many lessons, often in ways we do not expect. Some lessons come gently, like a whisper on the wind, while others arrive with the force of a storm. But each lesson, whether sweet or bitter, carries with it the potential for growth and understanding. The key is to embrace these lessons with an open heart, allowing them to shape and mold us into better versions of ourselves.

When we open our hearts to life's lessons, we move beyond mere survival to truly thriving. We begin to see that every experience, no matter how difficult, holds within it a seed of wisdom. These seeds, when nurtured, blossom into insights that guide us on our journey. They teach us about love, resilience, forgiveness, and the importance of living with purpose.

An open heart is also a heart willing to be vulnerable. It is through vulnerability that we connect most deeply with others and with ourselves. By embracing our own imperfections and acknowledging our fears, we open the door to profound personal growth. We learn that strength is not found in hiding our weaknesses but in accepting them and allowing them to teach us.

Moving Forward with Renewed Purpose

As we conclude this journey of reflection, healing, and growth, we find ourselves standing at the threshold of a new beginning. The tears we have shed, the lessons we have learned, and the healing we have experienced all point us toward a renewed sense of purpose. Moving forward, we are no longer burdened by the past but inspired by it. We carry with us the wisdom we've gained, the love we've shared, and the strength we've built.

This renewed purpose is not just about setting goals or achieving success; it is about living with intentionality and meaning. It is about choosing to live each day with an awareness of the preciousness of life, the fragility of time, and the importance of love and compassion. It is about making a conscious decision to use our experiences—both the joyful and the painful—to create a life that reflects our deepest values and desires.

Moving forward with renewed purpose also means continuing to grow and evolve. The journey of life is not a static one; it is dynamic, ever-changing, and full of opportunities for learning and transformation. With an open heart and a reflective spirit, we can navigate the challenges and opportunities that lie ahead with grace and courage.

Conclusion:
A Journey of Healing and Hope

In this book, we have explored the many facets of life's journey—the innocence of beginnings, the joy and pain of love, the seasons of friendship, the unseen scars we bear, the burden and blessing of responsibility, the quiet sorrow of regret, and the fragile beauty of time. We have delved into the silent battles within, the strength of faith in adversity, the legacy we leave behind, the beauty of letting go, and finally, the journey home.

Each chapter has been a step on the path toward healing and hope, a path that has led us to a deeper understanding of ourselves, our relationships, and our purpose in this world. As we close this book, let us carry forward the lessons we have learned, the insights we have gained, and the hope that has been rekindled in our hearts.

May the tears we have shed along the way be a source of healing, and may the hope that has been nurtured within us guide us as we continue our journey through life. With each step, may we walk with a renewed sense of purpose, embracing the beauty and the challenges of life with an open heart, and always moving forward with hope and love.

EPILOGUE

A MESSAGE TO MY YOUNGER SELF

Words of Wisdom from the Journey

Dear Younger Self,

As I reflect on the many twists and turns of life, I wish I could sit with you and share what I've learned along the way. Life, in all its beauty and complexity, is a journey that no one can truly prepare you for. The dreams you hold now will evolve, and the challenges you face will shape you in ways you cannot yet imagine. But take heart, for every experience—whether joyful or painful—carries with it a lesson that will guide you on the path to becoming who you are meant to be.

You will discover that life is not about avoiding hardships but about embracing them with courage and resilience. The trials you will encounter are not meant to break you but to refine you. With every setback, you will learn the value of perseverance. With every heartache, you will understand the depth of love. And with every loss, you will find new strength in the power of faith. Remember that growth often comes from discomfort, and it is in those moments of struggle that you will find your true self.

Encouragement for the Path Ahead

As you step forward into the unknown, know that you are never alone. There will be days when the road seems long and the weight of the world feels unbearable, but do not lose hope. Trust that every step you take, no matter how small, is moving you closer to the life you are meant to live. Your journey is uniquely yours, and it is unfolding exactly as it should.

When you encounter challenges that seem insurmountable, remember that you are stronger than you know. The courage you need is already within you, waiting to be discovered. Surround yourself with those who lift you up and believe in you, even when you struggle to believe in yourself. Lean on your faith, for it will be your anchor in times of uncertainty. And most importantly, never stop believing in the power of love—both the love you give and the love you receive.

A Blessing for the Future

As you look ahead to the life that awaits you, I offer you this blessing: May you walk in peace, knowing that every step of your journey is guided by a greater purpose. May you find joy in the simple moments, courage in the face of adversity, and wisdom in the lessons life will teach you. May your heart remain open to the beauty and wonder of the world, even when it feels heavy with sorrow. And may you always be surrounded by love, both from within and from those around you.

Your future is filled with endless possibilities, and the person you are becoming is someone of incredible strength, compassion, and grace. Embrace the journey with an open heart, and trust that you are exactly where you need to be.

With love and hope, Older Self

www.ingramcontent.com/pod-product-compliance
Lightning Source LLC
Chambersburg PA
CBHW051551010526
44118CB00022B/2665